I0152882

everything is somewhere

Also by Levenia Pretorius

Detention or Mindful?
School Readiness for Moms on the Go
The Good Book of Food Love & Wisdom

Levenia Pretorius

everything is somewhere

published by

Business Essentials

everything is somewhere. Copyright © 2021 by Levenia Pretorius. All rights reserved. Printed in South Africa. No part of this book may be used or reproduced in any manner whatsoever without written permission, except in the case of brief quotations embodied in critical articles and reviews. For information, address Business Essentials (Pty) Ltd - lp@forbusiness.co.za.

everything is somewhere may be purchased for educational, business, or sales promotional use.

Cover designed by Levenia Pretorius

The National Library of South Africa has catalogued the paperback and e-book edition as follows:

978-0-620-96837-9 (paperback)
978-0-620-96838-6 (e-book)

For my son, Carl.

A mother's love,
for her child, is impenetrable.

Anybody can have anything they want.

What if this is true?

If you do not like your life's results then change what you are doing. If you have problems in all areas of your life, then your thought pattern dictates your situation. You are doing something that gives a negative reaction.

What are your current results?

- What do you allow in your life?
- Who are you with?
- Who is in your immediate presence? Are they contributing positively or are they having a negative impact on your life?
- What is your behaviour?
- What assets do you have? Are they paid assets?
- What debt do you have?
- What savings do you have?
- Are people happy around you, and because of you?
- Are you happy?
- Are you a successful person - successful in your area of expertise?
- Are you at and in a place you really want to be?
- Do you have a pension fund in place which will give you a quality and dignified old age?

When you want something more, you have to change your thinking pattern, energy levels, attitude and vibration.

Stop smoking. Smoking clouds the mind and causes neurological damage in the brain. Stop excessive drinking. It damages the liver which affects your energy levels and affects your mood. Your body is poisoned and your pineal gland is clouded. The pineal gland is a tiny organ in the center of the brain.

Descartes, a French philosopher, regarded the pineal gland as the principal seat of the soul. It is the place in which all our thoughts are formed. To me, it is the throne of the soul. When your body is cleansed of ethanol, your soul is purified. Your body reverts to the positive vibrations you are created with.

Nobody can resist the beauty, innocence and vulnerability, of a new born baby, this pure and beautiful human. A baby has the most beautiful pure energy. We must strive to have this pure energy again.

When your body is purified, you can then make quality decisions. Your energy levels are up and you feel in control. When you have control, then you can command. The pineal gland is also viewed worldwide as the third eye as you can perceive (feel or detect) things not visible.

When your brain is intoxicated with ethanol or smoke then you are disconnected from what the Creator wants you to experience. You know what all the negative effects of drinking and smoking are and the financial cost of these bad habits.

Now some of you will immediately put the book down because nothing comes between you and your cigarettes or you and your drinking. But wait before you throw the book down. You are drinking to escape your troubles and your feelings. Your excessive drinking causes much trouble in your life. You do not know how to stop.
Everything is somewhere but you cannot find it with a clouded mind and intoxicated body. The universe does not vibrate like this.

We are soul and soul is perfect.

Do not cloud it with substances, as you disconnect your soul from finding perfection.

Sun Tsu said: "Those who wish to fight, must first count the cost. I say: "Those who wish to smoke and drink must first count the cost". Think about what smoking and drinking have cost you, financially and emotionally.

Think.

Make the list of what you have lost due to drinking.

Change. Save yourself.

If you are not experiencing positive results, then you have NOT learned anything.

We all need emotional help and the reason for it is paradigms. Paradigms are the deep-rooted convictions welded to our synapses. All our actions are filtered and regulated through these paradigms.

How do we change this?

It starts with thinking. Thinking is self-studying. Studying is also studying successful people, people who show real positive results and sustainable success. You have to keep on studying and expand your awareness. There is no quick fix.

Change is never comfortable. It takes real thinking and discovering the naked truth whether you have real deep respect for yourself.

Think deeply and intently about what new values to instill and have the discipline to stick to them.
Most of us read a book, then another and yet another but the fundamental lessons, the essence, does not sink in.

We hope to find a quick solution between some of the hundreds of sentences in a book. We need words to change our lives, but we are not willing to change how we think. Do we really understand what we read?

Do we think about what we read, the meaning, the lesson, and do we apply it?

Thinking is hard work.

Think quickly of what you said or texted to somebody just before you started reading this book. You said something to somebody. What was the person's reaction?
Think of what you did earlier today and what was the reaction you received?

Think of what you are going to do next and what will the reaction be.

Think deeply about why you are reading this book now.

Why did you choose to read this book?

Because you seek help. You seek a quick fix. Something which can give you a key to instant success, maybe a sentence that will inspire you.

We read a book, get instant motivation and say I will start changing my values tomorrow. We are on a high; we feel "Now that I have control of my life, I am going to have success". Then tomorrow comes and we do not feel the same high and the same motivation to get into action.

It is gone.

That is why our motivation is short-lived.

Think.

Understand.

Engage.

Commit.

Apply.

Re-commit.

Never quit.

Develop disciplined thinking. Think, every time, what the reaction will be before you say something or act in a certain way.

Read the page which resonates with you, over and over, until you understand it, and it becomes part of your soul. The application of knowledge will change you. No amount of knowledge will make you successful. It is the understanding and application thereof.

It is not enough to read an insightful book once and think you understand the content fully to apply it in your life.

Bob Proctor carries the book, "Think and grow rich", by Earl Nightingale, with him everywhere. He reads it every day. The wisdom conveyed in the book is part of Bob's DNA now. It guides him, it controls his thoughts and it helps him to think of every thought and action. Bob thinks about what he is thinking.

Bob Proctor is a high school dropout. After studying (not reading) "Think and Grow Rich", his mind was transformed. Today he is the CEO of Proctor Gallagher Institute. Bob Proctor's motto is "believing is seeing". You must believe before you will see anything happen in your life.

Have you ever believed, truly felt real believing, with your whole being?

Have you ever wanted something so much that you would do anything to get it and you would not quit? See? That is believing. You saw the result so vividly that nothing could distract you until you achieved what you saw in your mind's eye.

Believing creates order in your soul. It brings clarity to your life's path. Order is heaven's first law and those who have order, are in command.

Do you know what Abracadabra means?
Some theories include:

It is related to another magical word - 'abraxas'. In the Greek system of alphabetic numerology, this word is significant in that it contains letters that add up to 365, the number of days in the year. The word is of Hebrew or Aramaic origin, being derived either from the Hebrew words 'ab' (father), 'ben' (son), and 'ruach hakodesh' (holy spirit), or from the Aramaic 'avra kadavra', meaning 'it will be created in my words'.
Magicians use the word 'abracadabra'. This means 'I create as I speak'.

Words create. You say, "I love you", then you create a relationship and you even create an emotion, called affection, for yourself and the receiver of the words.

Use positive words as they have a vibration and will attract wealth, happiness, and sustainable prosperity to your life.

Words make or break. What you say becomes. Everything you want and need is somewhere. You have to believe it first, and then you will see it.

A good friend of mine once told me:
"What you do not know, you will not recognise."

When the magician performs, all looks like magic to you. It is trickery. Once you are behind the scenes to see how the magician performs his tricks, then your ignorance disappears.

So once you know, ignorance disappears. Knowledge comes through words. Words come from books and wise people.

Reading opens up universes in your mind; it makes you strong and courageous. Studying successful people shows you the path traveled by courageous people is possible. A path you can also embark upon. It will not be easy but you will make it if you follow the laws of the universe.

I hope that this book will embed new knowledge in your mind, spur you on to understand the information and to apply it, to benefit you greatly.

In this book, I will share some of the wisdom I shared in my book, "The Good Book of Food, Love & Wisdom". Along with critical thinking, setting boundaries, believing, and seeing what I wanted (visualisation) gave me the strength to lift my chin, and face each day towards a better future. The power of visualisation is not mumbo jumbo. It is truly believing something and by doing this, your energy will match the giving nature of the universe.

Most people on earth drift through their days without knowing themselves and the vehicle (body) they are in. I showed a picture of the brain to a group of teachers and asked them to name all the parts and their respective functions. The most they could identify were three parts. These people have to teach children but do not know their brain parts nevermind knowing the functions thereof.

The point is, we want to go through life with joy but do not understand what is happening inside of our brain. I wanted to be wealthy, have abundance so as not to worry about my retirement. Sometimes I was questioning my efforts and my purpose in life. Why, despite all my efforts, hard work and good intentions, was I NOT creating sustainable wealth? My questions lead me to watch interviews on Youtube with wealthy people and I detected a common thread.

What it was that they had or did, which made them sustainably wealthy?

1. They are thinkers. They think about their behaviour and they visualise what they want, really want, and do not quit. Most have a vision board.

2. They have realistic goals. They do not go after money and do good with their goods or service. They have a meaningful purpose.

3. They read inspiring books on success and apply precisely what is prescribed.

4. They raise their vibrational frequency to that which they want.

5. They have multiple money-earning ideas.

6. They save and invest their money wisely.

7. They never procrastinate.

8. They set emotional, physical, and financial boundaries.

9. They understand that they are here on earth to be grateful and to have unconditional love.

10 They understand that motivation is a symptom and not a solution, that engaging is a spontaneous action, when you love what you are doing.

The most powerful being is YOU. You can find anything that you look for, realistically, if you believe.
Imitation is suicide. Be yourself. Yes, you cannot change, but by changing the quality of your values, your life WILL change for the better. Sometimes slowly but it WILL!
Write down what your current values are. How does it impact your life? Is it a positive or negative impact?

Believe in yourself. The greatest success is being yourself. Think critically about what you are doing and how you are doing it. You can only believe in yourself when you have connected with each of your actions and have a clear vision of what you want and where you are going.
Play songs and words that will train your mind to think more positively. The subconscious mind looks at whatever you give it to look at. What do you feed your subconscious mind?

> "Most people tip-toe through life, hoping they make it safely to death". Bob Proctor

If any person thinks that they will be happy all the time, then they are disillusioned. Dr. Demartini did a study on his emotional ups and downs for two years and found his ups and downs canceled each other out. So, it is okay to have downs, as the ups will be equal.

To understand your life and to be happy, you have to have balanced thinking.

Understand that sometimes you will be happy, sometimes less happy, and sometimes just downright sad or depressed. You can alter the depth of these emotions by having your sticky note affirmations around you and alter the inner voice by feeding your mind with positive information. When you feel depressed, focus your mind on your priorities and work on your goals. Deviate your mind and when you look again you have achieved something for the day and you feel better. Even if it is just de-cluttering a cupboard. It always works.
If you do not govern yourself, then the world will govern you. Embrace both sides of life and you will be prepared for the real world.

I need to tell my story because I am so grateful for the miracles in my life. The circumstances at my house, when I was only 10 years of age, were horrific. We were taken away from alcoholic parents and placed into foster care. My dad occasionally beat my mom. This was besides the parties and the fights amongst the drunken men. Our electricity was cut off and we had to use an extension cord to get electricity from our neighbours. The surrounding neighbours gave food when they could but became fed-up with helping as my parents did not try to improve our situation. Things were very bad.

My dad left and came back sometime just before we were taken away by the social services.
I assume my dad had to come back as the creditors took everything away from us and he had to sign for our release to the social worker.

I do not think that my parents cried when we four children left for the final time. They stood there, doing nothing. Nothing. Did not fight to keep us, did not change, and did not care. I could almost see a sense of relief in them. I wonder till today, how they slept that evening. Did they think of us? Did they get drunk again? They never came to fetch us. They never came to save us.
In the end, I am so happy they did not. My parents would never have been able to give me the quality of

life, the education, and finishing I received. They did not have the emotional capability to do so. They could not even help themselves!

We were placed with a woman and her husband who had three children of their own, had already had a problem foster child, and there we were, four unwanted children. Eight children in a house. I disliked the woman the moment I saw her. I am sure she looked into my eyes and disliked me too. Being age 11, left no room to make my own decisions. I was emotionally battered by this woman and eventually she made me sleep in the garage, like a dog. The only beautiful thing in the garage was the rain falling hard on the zinc roof, draining away some of the loneliness and carrying me into a dreamless sleep.

Luckily, foster care, too, did not work out for me.
I landed at interim foster parents before being sent to a children's home. In the room, was a cupboard. Glued inside the door was a tattered piece of laminated paper. The words on this old paper changed my outlook on life.

Amid utmost turmoil, hurt, and feelings of rejection this was the moment when my future's door opened. Through fate, it was on this cupboard door.

Promise Yourself

To be so strong that nothing can disturb your peace of mind. To talk health, happiness, and prosperity to every person you meet.

To make all your friends feel that there is something in them. To look at the sunny side of everything and make your optimism come true.

To think only the best, to work only for the best and to expect only the best. To be just as enthusiastic about the success of others as you are about your own.

To forget the mistakes of the past and press on to the greater achievements of the future. To wear a cheerful countenance at all times and give every living creature you meet a smile.

To give so much time to the improvement of yourself that you have no time to criticize others. To be too large for worry, too noble for anger, too strong for fear, and too happy to permit the presence of trouble.

To think well of yourself and to proclaim this fact to the world, not in loud words but great deeds. To live in faith that the whole world is on your side so long as you are true to the best that is in you."

Christian D. Larson, Your Forces and How to Use Them

Every paragraph inspired and encouraged me. Thirty years later I had the opportunity to share these words with hundreds of children from less privileged backgrounds, on the front page of a literacy development workbook. Hoping that some of the words would open doors, heal some wounds in their innocent minds and let a beautiful future in, despite their dire circumstances.

"There is always one moment in childhood when the door opens and lets the future in."
Graham Greene, "The Power and the Glory"

Looking back at my life, I made some horrible mistakes. I am asking myself whether I am stupid, naive, or just a weak person. How I wished and wish that I had and have a guide to help me in each challenging and life-changing situation. I wished for wisdom and knowledge, to make life easy, pleasurable, and without any emotional pain.

Today, I know this: Life does not come with a manual. The Creator gave us a brain and we do not use it. We do not think because we were not taught how to think. And if we know, then we are too lazy to think.
For today I know that boundaries for myself make life easier and less painful.

Through much hardship, I have learned how to set my boundaries. Doing this, has given me time to start writing, creating books with a purpose.

The purpose of these books is to share wisdom with others which they will hopefully apply in their lives to make life a joy or at least give them some hope that their situation can improve if they start thinking about their current behaviour and how to set strict boundaries.

What gave me solid hope was that everything is somewhere. You just have to go and search for it. Thinking has given me the hope that I can make quality choices again and put my life back on track.

I started researching what makes people land up in the situations they are in, such as depression, anger, bitterness, developing illnesses, overeating, over-drinking, and financial and emotional bankruptcy.

My research brought me to persons such as Dr. Joe Dispenza. In my distress, he was the only person who made sense to me and gave me real guidance as to how to understand my situation and know that I am ultimately responsible for the change. Unfortunately, I was the only one who could change ME. I needed to know what to do to improve my circumstances.

I was starting to get this nudge to want to share my story with people. I realised that I am not the only one with problems. I did not want to change because I thought that my problem was unique, that the universe, after all, designed it for me specifically, for me only. I cannot let go of this problem! I was addicted to the pain and suffering mentality, and the worst of it all was that I thought I did not deserve any better because I was not good enough.

We all know how it feels to be betrayed by somebody you trusted wholeheartedly. Maybe it was a romantic partner, maybe a friend or a colleague.

What if you betrayed yourself?

We betray ourselves when we know what the correct thing to do is, and we don't do it, or we try, fail, and give up. We want to start exercising, we want to lose weight, eat healthier, stop smoking, stop drinking, read more or stop bad behavior. We begin by being so motivated, and we think, "NOW we are going to get it right". We do it for an hour, a day, or maybe even a week and then we are back to the old thoughts, old choices, past behavior and old emotions. The emotions of guilt, feelings of, "I am not good enough", "I am a failure" and "Why even try?".

You feed yourself excuses such as, "I am too much like my mom, my dad", "I am too weak" or, "I will start tomorrow".

If you respond to that thought as if it is true, then that same thought will lead to the same choice, which will lead to the same behavior, which will create the same experience, which will lead to the same emotions. So the body becomes the mind. That is why most people cannot succeed in making lasting changes in their lives. But there is something that works IF you stick to it and IF you will be brutally honest with yourself.

We are so addicted to the emotions of the past. The moment we do something different, the body says, "oooh, oooh what is going on here, this is not feeling right, this is not what I am used to doing". Your body is on autopilot. By the time we reach age 35, we have a software program that we find very difficult to delete.

It is being on auto pilot.

The autopilot looks like this. The first thing in the morning, we grab our phones, check WhatsApps, SMS, Facebook, Instagram, LinkedIn, Pinterest, Twitter, E-mails, and Snapchat. We check the news, take a photo of our first cup of coffee or the sunrise and post it on Facebook, and now we feel connected to what is familiar to us.

Then we have routine behavior. We get out of bed the same side, go to the bathroom, make coffee, get dressed, drive to work via the same route, see the same people, the same people who are annoying us and this becomes like a software program running in the background, day in and day out. We lose our FREE will. We need this software program, and we are addicted to it.

We wake up in the morning thinking of all our past and not-even-happened-yet problems, day in and day out. We do not like our jobs, our children are giving us a hard time and our spouses are giving us a hard time.

As I proceeded with my research, I realised I needed to change because I did not want to be the person I had become.

I had this deep URGE to reinvent myself, to have a new personality, a new experience and new circumstances. For this evolution to take place in me, the following action needed to be taken. I had to develop new thoughts, a new thinking pattern.

- Thinking new thoughts would lead to new and better quality choices.
- New choices would lead to new behavior.
- New behavior creates new emotions.

- New emotions would give me renewed energy.
- Renewed energy would enable me to grasp new
  opportunities.
- New opportunities would make me reach the goals I
  have set for myself.
- Achieving goals would make me feel happy and strive
  to achieve more of my goals.

If you always do what you repetitively have done, then
you will still get what you always got.

Think of your programmed thought pattern and
habitual behaviour. Write it down and you will realise
with shock that it is YOU who causes whatever is not
right in your life.

YOU can change it by thinking of your actions and
mindfully acting positively. It starts by thinking and the
Creator gave us this ability for free. Carpe Diem.

What do you want different in your life?

It starts with a thought. Make sure it is the thought you
want.

Repeat that thought over and over again, every day.
Start with it in the morning and sleep with that thought
in your head, like a mantra. A mantra is a Sanskrit word,

having the power to change one's behavior or an outcome. The secret is to repeat it, believe it, and never quit.

Say, for instance, you want to write a book, and then you repeat to yourself a million times in the day, "I can write a book." I have used an elastic band around my wrist, and every time I had a negative thought, I would pull the elastic band and hit myself hard. Through this, I have eradicated negative thoughts.

Doubt and unnecessary thoughts still try to sabotage my efforts, but I can put them out of my head more effortlessly and more rapidly.

Thoughts that are embedded, are, "I am good enough" and "I am worth achieving my goals and being happy".

Through this, I created new neural pathways in my brain.

YOU AND ONLY YOU HAVE THE POWER TO CHANGE YOUR THOUGHT PATTERN

After my research, I made an effort to reinvent myself. When I say reinvent myself, I mean that I changed my thought pattern completely.

I now know that there is not somebody out there with a remote control changing my emotions. I am the only one who can change them by changing my thoughts and by forcing myself to think of positive outcomes.

I guided my thoughts by looking at my motivational sticky notes whenever I felt a negative nudge appear. I wake up every morning and ask how I can become the best version of myself today. I think of ten things to be grateful for. I do not climb out of bed before I have thought about the ten things. Then I apply my energy to think of the positive outcomes for the day and try to achieve the tasks and goals I wrote down the previous evening before I went to sleep. I keep a notebook next to my bed.

I make my to-do list and look at my goals and ensure I do not waste precious time on 'voyeur-ing' other people on Facebook, but instead investing this time on myself and my goals. THIS WORKS!

Sit down, without your cellphone, and analyse what you are feeling. I listen to what my feelings are saying. What are the emotions telling me? What are they feeding me to believe? Why are those thoughts in my head? Use this table below to change that harmful software program continually running in your subconscious mind.

What feelings are dwelling in me every day?	What are those feelings saying to me?	Why are those feelings here? What event happened for the emotions to dwell in me?	What am I going to say to myself instead? What do I have to do to get rid of these negative feelings?	What will the outcome be, once I have changed this? How will I feel? How will my life be?

I started to experience what I was feeling, what these feelings were telling me. These feelings dictated HOW I felt and WHAT to think and HOW to act.

I became aware that Goodness was around me, and I needed to tap into it with my feelings, thoughts, and actions. I realised that the general sense I had acquired and was feeling was negative. I doubted myself and it prevented me from experiencing greatness. Although I tried hard to motivate myself to think positively and tap into the Goodness around me, the underlying 'voice' that I heard was ALWAYS negative.

"It is never going to happen, you are not good enough, what do you think you are doing in trying this, you know you always make mistakes."

These are the messages which were always in my chest area. Yes, I felt and heard it from my chest. It made me extremely curious why these feelings were dwelling there. It was like a software program running in the background for most of my adult life.

I realised with a shock that I was going through my daily life without listening to my feelings. I did not take note of the impact they had on my decision-making and my mood. My curiosity led me to discover the chakras, the energy centers of the body.

The feelings of negativity and profound self-doubt came from my heart chakra or energy center.

I was going through great turbulence in my life. Events happened which were out of my control and threw me off course.
I went through severe trauma and caused my heart physical pain. Pain that I could feel in my chest, along with all the excessive crying and confusion.
My body's DNA memorized the pain as it was intense trauma and started to replay the events which had caused the pain. Maybe my body was trying to protect

me from more pain and kept on reminding me by putting these feelings forward to warn me not to get hurt again.

I explored the heart chakra or Anahata (in Sanskrit, Anahata means "unhurt, unstruck, and unbeaten"), situated in the center of the chest. Meaning unhurt in Sanskrit, Anahata relates to the love energy in the body. When in balance, we feel love, compassion, and forgiveness.

I had none of the above in my heart. I had to forgive so much. I was hurt so much. I felt beaten in all ways. As I write this book, I feel beaten. An event in my life caused me to try and fight a system but I was defeated. I could not and cannot win.

I had to let go and let TIME fix whatever was not possible for me to fix. Even though I thought that I had forgiven those who hurt me, I had not. I still experienced a bitter hate taste in my mouth. I had to let go of this oppressive feeling to become in balance with all my energy centers. I had to rid myself of that deep resentment. I had to check what I was feeling and analyze it continually.
I needed to hear what the feelings were saying to me and align myself with Goodness. The STOP technique helped me whenever I listened to the negative talk.

Read more about the STOP technique further in the book.

I started making motivational sticky notes with words such as "feeling good will make it good". Positive thoughts became my road map (referring to using my mind to think forward to my goals). It is like training a muscle and the motivational sticky notes will remind you not to give up.

It is not possible for you to feel positive and for things to turn out badly. Nor is it possible for you to feel negative and have a positive outcome. The way you feel will tell you exactly where you are heading and if you are in tune with Goodness that is always there. Goodness does not appear when you think of it. It is all around you and is there for you to tap into and align yourself with positive energy!

Only your emotions restrict you from accessing Goodness. Your feelings influence your actions. Your actions will determine how you will feel again.
For instance, if you decide to abuse alcohol because a loved one has mistreated you, then you are going to feel bad afterwards. Your emotions allowed this feeling to cause you to sink into even more bad feelings. So the cycle repeats. You have to say to yourself that you deserve goodness and tap into it and make quality

choices. Quality choices will catapult you into greater feelings and experiences.

Dr. Joe Dispenza - the one person who makes sense to me

I discovered Dr. Joe Dispenza in my frantic search on Google for answers as to why I landed in this situation, why I was experiencing negative feelings. Maybe it was more searching for help than anything else, as I did not want to go and see a therapist.

Dr. Joe is my modern-day hero as he made it so easy to understand what was going on in my brain and why I was acting this way. It was as if somebody stood at my side, took a deep breath, and blew off the thick dust which was covering the surface of my mind.

By going in-depth with my studies about his teachings, I started understanding what had happened to me. I was hanging on to thoughts of my past so that I could not use my healthy mind as a map to my new future. When that happened, things in my life started changing rapidly.
My goals became clear to me. Most importantly, I could not waste time on people or things that were not contributing to my success and well-being.

As my mindset changed, events happened, which caused me to end false and toxic relationships.

I changed where I was living and I changed my routine. I wrote this book, my fourth. I managed to set boundaries for myself and others. I managed to set financial, physical and emotional boundaries for myself and for others who had managed to consume me, my resources and time. Most of all, I realised the power of my own 'NO'. Saying a clear 'NO' to people gave me back the ability to control my life and to live it the way I wanted to.

It was not always easy, as deep down in me; I still wanted to be a people pleaser. But, I realised that this would get me nowhere and the other person was the only one enjoying the benefit.

I would love to give you more background about a man who I know has a clear understanding of human beings. To me, Dr. Joe Dispenza knows how to provide tools to help oneself sustainably!

Dr. Joe Dispenza is a neuroscientist and chiropractor, author and educator. His message is that each of us has the potential for greatness and unlimited abilities. Watching his interviews on YouTube, it is easy to understand and apply the knowledge he shares.

Everything he says is scientifically proven and makes sense to anybody who has the desire to want to change their day-to-day experience and outcome. One of Dr. Joe Dispenza's most important messages, which also helped me, was to use your brain like a road map for the future.

Dr. Joe Dispenza did a study on people with cancer who healed themselves, and all of them had four things in common

1.   They realised they were riding on the back of a giant. That they were not alone.
2.   They understood that their thoughts contributed to their condition.
3.   They reinvented themselves. They asked the question, "What if?"
4.   They spent time alone, secluded. They took the time to meditate.

We blame events of the past for the situations we are experiencing. People make excuses for why they cannot move forward blaming an event that happened in their past. Excuses such as "I am this way because he cheated on me five years ago!" or "I am this way because my dad was an abusive alcoholic 20 years ago."

We blame events in our past for justifying why we are the way we are. That is why we cannot change, BUT do we want to change? It is too comfortable to stay the way we are. It is also easy to fall back into our old patterns. Do you know that you can use your brain as a map to the future? What I did was, every time I had a negative thought or did not want to do something positive towards my goals, I thought forward.
Thinking forward means seeing yourself achieving the goal or visualising how you completed the tasks. This visualisation secretes the neurotransmitter, dopamine, to give you the energy to do the task at hand. Focus your attention on your goals the moment a negative thought creeps in.

Set your alarm an hour earlier and go to bed an hour later. You have gained two hours a day. Stop going out with friends for a while. Regain lost time and wasted opportunities by working extra hours a day. Make up for the wasted time and your precious resources, given to insignificant people. The time you could have spent working on value-adding projects to assist in building up a pension. Before you know it, you are older and have not put away enough money for retirement. Have you sat down and calculated what you would receive at age 55 or 65 for a pension? Have you spoken to your broker to give you an accurate picture of how your financial situation will look at age 55? How old are you now and how much have you been putting away?

I got the biggest shock of my life when I realised that I would not have enough for my old age. This thought made me realise how much time and resources I have spent on insignificant friendships and activities. How I lost precious things in my life which I had worked so hard for and which would have made a difference in my old age. They are gone now. Now I have to make up for lost time.

The ill advice I took from greedy people, investments and decisions I have made to feed their greed, cost me my assets. In the end, it was me standing alone, me standing without anything, me who had to start from scratch. Me, who lost precious time.

Do not give your time and resources for instant pleasure or relationships which seem genuine but will never be. If had I only followed the advice of Carl Sandburg earlier in my life:

"Time is the coin of your Life. It is the only coin you have, and only you can determine how it will be spent. Be careful lest you let other people spend it for you; and when you spend it, spend it wisely so that you get the most for your expenditure." Carl August Sandburg

A few other tips to help you to get out of your blocks and unlock your mental blocks

USE YOUR BRAIN AS A ROAD MAP FOR THE FUTURE

Negativity does not skip anybody. The only way to overcome this is to have a clear picture of whom and what you want to become. How you want to feel and what you want to achieve. When you are sinking into that hole that your own emotions dragged you into, then immediately focus your attention on that picture you have of your future self.

Put sticky notes on your mirror, fridge, car and front door with those goals (your road map). Some people hide their sticky notes when people come to visit. Do not hide them. Be an inspiration to others to also put sticky notes up. You are not weak when you have a physical display of encouraging words. Your motivational sticky notes might just as well be the very words that another person needs.

THE 5-SECOND RULE

I use The 5-Second Rule of Mel Robbins when I feel that I want to lie in my bed longer. This rule is so easy and effective. All you do is to block out everything negative you feel and count 5, 4, 3, 2, 1, and UP.

Once you are up, get out of the room, switch on the light.

Go to the spot where you have all your goals written down and review the list. Then go back to your room, make your bed, and start your day with new vigour. A day where you are one step nearer to your goals. Achieving your goals is a product of everyday dedication, every day taking that one step in the right direction and every day reading your motivational sticky notes.

Eventually, it will stick!

TIME POCKETS

I do this and it works so well. I also taught my son this technique because some school tasks can be so overwhelming. I showed him that he should use the 10-minute-time-pocket technique. For every awful task you have to do, tell yourself that you will start and do this task for ten minutes or have to complete this in ten minutes. You can break up the whole task into ten-minute pockets.

Your cellphone is not in this activity for checking WhatsApp or Facebook. Set your phone on flight mode so that Whatsapps do not come through. In this dedicated ten minutes, your phone is used as a timer. Every cellphone has a stopwatch. So use it.

Focus on the task at hand and start doing the activities. Some tasks will feel like having to untie a ball of knotted wool. But once you have started, it will get easier and the challenge will make you feel good and even better once you have achieved it. After ten minutes you can stand up and drink water and then come back and focus for just another ten minutes. Before you know it, you will have completed the task.

My son was very despondent about a school project he had to do. It was during the COVID-19 lockdown and he was very negative. He applied the 10-minute-time-pocket technique and came back after completing the task and said, "That was not so bad after all".

You can overcome any task by taking ten minutes at a time and focusing, without answering WhatsApp or Facebook in between. Put your phone on flight mode.

THE STOP SIGN

Have you thought about where negative thoughts originate?

1. Negative thoughts come from past failures embedded in your memory

Remember what Dr. Joe Dispenza suggests?
You can use your mind as a map for a positive future.
Every time you have a negative thought or

procrastinate, then think of your goals. Think of what you want to achieve. See how you are achieving it. Feel the feelings of how it would feel once you have achieved the goal or completed the task. Every human being's situation will differ from the next, and by no means am I making your situation out as insignificant. Some of you might be dealing with the loss of a beloved.

Emotions do become less hurtful as time passes. But while you are allowing them to take control of your life, it might be very destructive. My sincerest desire is to lessen the pain and shorten the period of this intense emotional hurting, for others. I truly wish I could take away emotional hurting for people as this is one of the most challenging emotions to deal with.

I had to go through excruciating pain. I lost a loved one. I experienced the most profound betrayal from a person I trusted and I am shameful of my past. So I am not giving this advice from my comfort or never-got-hurt zone.

To ease the hurt, I am using my mind, daily, as a map to the future. I have experienced this during times when I want to sink into more negativity and procrastination. I focus my thoughts on the map for my future. My sticky notes help me to focus on my goals and my motivational quotes. Do not think people are going to believe you are weak when they see your sticky notes. Remember that you will stay weak without them!

2. It comes from comparing yourself to other people's so-called success

Comparison creates the emotion, "I am not good enough", which we all experience.

Yes, some people work just as hard as you do, and even harder, to achieve what they have achieved. These are people who did not compare themselves to others and who worked harder from the convictions in their hearts. They had positive quotes they wrote on paper and maybe even sticky notes. They did not falter in seeing their road map to a better future.
These people got back on track when they took a wrong turn (procrastination and self-doubt). People who persisted, even though they still thought that they were weak and worthless. It started making sense to them that the harder they worked, the more confident they became. The more sticky notes, with positive quotes and your main goals, which are around you, the quicker your time to get out of negativity and reach your goals.

3. Unfortunately, it also comes from something somebody said in the past or just blaming your past

We all had that one day when somebody said something about us, or to us, and for some reason, it stuck. You cannot get rid of it. You blame your past for how you are now. Your past has nothing to do with your NOW.
Yesterday is gone. Today has nothing to do with the past. The two periods can never be connected again. So move forward.

Only your thoughts are the connection to the past. You can blame your past for how you are now, or you can put your sticky notes up and apply your beautiful mind to navigating your road map to a positive and peaceful future. Use the sticky notes to be the GPS's guiding voice to your destination. When you use a GPS, the voice is quick to say, "Turn around when possible," when you are going in the wrong direction.

Use the sticky notes as a voice to re-route yourself to go in the right direction. It is acceptable to accidentally go in the wrong direction (procrastination or self-doubt). You will find that you get back on the right track more quickly, as you apply these techniques. In the beginning, it will be difficult and even annoying as your brain is so used to the brain path which you have been travelling all your life.

4. Then as that negative thought to want to procrastinate enters your mind, see how you lift this big stop sign and say 'STOP'

Do not allow your thoughts to enable you to procrastinate. For example, to go back to bed or not do a specific task. It gets easier the moment you get that picture of the STOP sign in your mind. Negative thoughts are created in your mind. They swell up from all the years of allowing negative thoughts to engulf you because you have not used any mind techniques to stop these thoughts.

It is easier to dwell on your circumstances due to your past. It is easier to blame the past and others than to take responsibility and action to stop what is happening to you. Lift that STOP sign and say "STOP" and then look at your sticky notes. Soon after you have started your sticky notes, it will pop up in your mind automatically. It will be embedded in your DNA. You cannot have the same thoughts again.

Nobody cares if you have not achieved your goals and only a few people are truly happy when you do, and then they soon, too, forget your success. Ultimately the goals you achieve impact the quality of YOUR life, YOUR future and only YOU can determine in which direction you are going. Use the sticky notes as the GPS voice and head towards a more rewarding and meaningful life.

Now, let us get to what you need to become sustainably wealthy and happy. I will guide you through the most important must-do's to become sustainably wealthy and be happy.

Visualise what you want and really want it and do not quit. Have a vision board.
Everything that is real, was imagined first.

Everything is created twice. Once in your mind and once in life.

"Your mindset is a magnet. If you think of blessings, you attract blessings. If you think of problems, you attract problems. Always cultivate good thoughts and always remain optimistic. We get what we think, so think positive, life will be automatically positive". Bob Proctor

The most famous, rich, and successful people have a vision board and are not shy to talk about it.

Oprah Winfrey visualised her role in the movie "The Colour Purple". She read the book and knew in her heart that the role of Sophia was hers. When she saw that Steven Spielberg and Quincy Jones were producing a movie of the book, she started telling everybody she was going to act in the movie. After being rejected at the auditions and ending up going to a fat farm, because she thought she was too fat, she received a phone call from Steven Spielberg telling her she had the role. Her visualisation pulled her to the role.

Jim Carrey wrote himself a cheque for $10 million and gave himself 5 years and dated it for Thanksgiving 1995 He kept it safe in his wallet, where it was deteriorating. He would visualise directors saying that they liked his work. Although he had nothing, the words he was repeating made him feel better.

He would visualise that he had everything, that it was out there, within his reach.

Every night he would drive up Mullholland Drive. The road offers breathtaking views of the Los Angeles Basin, the San Fernando Valley, Downtown Los Angeles and the Hollywood Sign. The road has some of the most expensive homes in the world.
Just before Thanksgiving, he was offered the part in Dumb and Dumber for $10 million. In an interview with

Oprah, she asked Jim Carrey, whether visualisation works when you work hard, his answer was, "Well, yeah, That's the thing, you can't just visualise and then, you know, go eat a sandwich."

"The ruling mental state is everything. Our inner faculties are where it's really happening. Not outside of us. What you think produces your life". Bob Proctor

You are the architect of your destiny.

You are supported by the universe. You don't have to wonder what you're going to get. You'll get everything you'll ever need. Just focus on controlling the flow and what you can give. That's the way it works.

Follow the following steps to make sure you're using visualisation, or what I like to call visioneering, effectively: Cut pictures from a magazine and glue them to a board. Your wants must be realistic. The money you want to earn must be honest and through hard and clever work. You must serve other people. You cannot just receive. Your vision board must be balanced with giving and receiving.
The voice is telling you that you are not good enough, not pretty enough, not rich enough, not smart enough. It is the constant negative voice, in your head, which keeps talking in the background. Think for a moment.

You are not good enough compared to whom? Are you constantly comparing yourself to people who are also fighting their negative thoughts?

This belief system, which has been embedded over the years, should be deleted.

People who also think their noses are too big or their faces are too round. The first step to recovery and inner peace is to accept yourself because others also have their internal battles and constant negative debates.

People in their luxury cars are showcasing that they have money or exhausting debt for that car. A German luxury car gets from point A to B in the same way, on the same road, as a small Japanese car. See the analogy here?
We all have to travel on the same "road" because we are human. The German car does not have an exclusive superior road because it is a luxury car. It also has to stop at the traffic light and can only go when the light is green. Maybe it can travel faster, but the person driving the car has most probably more debt, and the fuel usage is more.
The one in the small Japanese car travels light and has less debt. So do not compare your life to others. Create your internal peace, and from that wisdom will come and a peaceful life.

Travel light.

A significant percentage of the global population who have huge houses, have a mortgage. A study has shown that people in these large houses utilise only 15% of the total space. What are they showcasing? That they enjoy the spaciousness, or that they can afford a huge property? Will they, publically, admit what total debt they have? No, they will not. What more are they showing through it? What is your answer?

Do they have inner peace and real joy because of all the debt? No. Short-lived joy was brought about by obtaining the luxury car, taking the drugs, having the nose job, boob job, or the new garment.
Warren Buffet is still living in the same house he bought in 1958. I am not saying, do not buy or build your dream home. I am telling you from experience not to buy more "home" than you can afford.

Is it not a goal, while we are on Earth, to live a worry-free existence? A life without the emotional burden of back-breaking debt and worries? I am not suggesting that you should not buy a house on credit. Does this debt take your joy away? I am not saying that you should not buy your dream car. I am asking YOU, what are the things which take away your joy?

We deserve a life with love and peace around us but mostly inner peace to be able to deal with the turmoil and promote self-acceptance.

Real joy is the moment when you walk in a mall, not feeling self-conscious, knowing that you are good enough and in precisely the same boat as the other people in the crowd.

Maybe even better off. Each person has their own set of problems, challenges and insecurities, and having compassion for them, makes you more comfortable in yourself.

Even the best-dressed person in the mall or crowd has their fair share of unhappiness and turmoil. So do not be quick to judge people who look as if they are better off than you. There is a song which was very popular in the 90s and I loved it. The song describes our situation so perfectly. Maybe you will remember the song, The Seven Nation Army, with the lyrics:

"Don't wanna hear about it
Every single one's got a story to tell
Everyone knows about it
From the Queen of England to the hounds of Hell."

Bob Proctor writes his goals or positive affirmations on a piece of paper and puts it in his pocket. This connects him to his words. This is how he became one of the great achievers in the world.

Earl Nightingale advises us to sit down and think deeply about what it is we really want. You will not know until you have been there, failed, and gone back, again and again. Sir Edmund Hillary reached Mount Everest after 12 attempts.
If you have not been there, done that, and got the T-shirt, then you do not know. The people, who made the mistakes and learned from them, will know the best.

Motivation is not a solution. It is a method to get people to do what they must do, or what you want them to do, because they do not really want to do it.

When you are engaged (committed and really want it) then you do not need motivation. You will not take a break and you will not stop until you have it.

Have realistic goals. Do not go after money but strive for the purpose.

"If it scares you, it might be a good thing to try".
Seth Godin

Set goals which are you.

Not fantasies.

Write down what you want, in as much detail as possible.

Write your worthy goal on a piece of paper and keep it in your pocket every day. Look at it several times a day, until you have reached your goal. Then go on to the next one.

You will have to work hard to achieve your goals. Nobody says it will be easy, but it is achievable if you stick to the process. Be relaxed about your goals and see in your mind's eye how you have already achieved them.

> In the New Testament of the Bible, Galatians 6:7 is written: "Do not be deceived, God is not mocked; for whatever a man sows, this he will also reap."

What you put into action now will manifest later. Positive or negative. We are the sum total of our thoughts. We must control our thoughts. We must think about what we think about.

If you sow positive thoughts then your life will be filled with positive things. The opposite is also real.
Why do men with goals succeed and keep on succeeding and men without goals, do not? We become what we think about. If you think of nothing you become nothing.

Goals give order to your life. Goals are like a magnet that pulls you up and makes you not want to give up. You can alter your life when you alter your thought pattern and are disciplined about it. Keep thinking positively, believe, keep trying and do not give up. If you care about and deeply connect with your goal then you will certainly attain it.

"Use your imagination to create mental movies of your desired goal". Bob Proctor

When you go after just the money, you will quit as soon as you start. Your goal must serve your highest values, serve others and give a positive vibration to others and the universe.
Accept what happened to you. (It is what it is.) Harvest the good. (There is good in everything). Find it. Forget the rest, and VISUALIZE what's next!

A goal chart helps me to plot all my goals and to pull me more quickly towards achieving them. I see the goals every day and the chart holds me accountable to achieve them.

Striving towards your goals and thinking about them in times when you are down, lonely, and have no motivation, will help to spur you on again. Thinking of your goals makes the brain secrete endorphins which will start making you feel more happy and positive.

Goal setting will occupy your mind and take your mind off thinking of loneliness and failure. It will give you a purpose in life. It works. Try it. Whenever you feel down again, immediately think of your goals. Experience how your feelings change and how your body reacts.

The Goal Chart

The chart has two sides. Your goals on the left and a date by which to achieve them, on the right-hand side. Challenging yourself to achieve the goals on the date you have written. Everyone loves a challenge.

They read books on success and do precisely what is prescribed.

You already have everything you need to succeed locked up inside you. Reading and studying simply draw out and develop that what's already within. It empowers you to be your best self.

Reading expands your awareness.

Below are a few books which I can recommend. Please note that the reviews are not all my own words and credit to the sources is given at the back of this book.

Think and Grow Rich - Earl Nightingale

"Think and Grow Rich" has been called the "Granddaddy of All Motivational Literature." It was the first book to boldly ask, "What makes a winner?" The man who asked and listened for the answer, Napoleon Hill, is now counted in the top ranks of the world's winners himself. The most famous of all teachers of success spent "a fortune and the better part of a lifetime of effort" to produce the "Law of Success" philosophy that forms the basis of his books and that is so powerfully summarized in this one.

In the original "Think and Grow Rich", published in 1937, Hill draws on stories of Andrew Carnegie, Thomas Edison, Henry Ford, and other millionaires of his generation to illustrate his principles. In the updated version, Arthur R. Pell, Ph.D., a nationally known author, lecturer, and consultant in human resources management and an expert in applying Hill's thought, deftly interweaves anecdotes of how contemporary millionaires and billionaires, such as Bill Gates, Mary Kay Ash, Dave Thomas, and Sir John Templeton, achieved their wealth. Outmoded or arcane terminology and examples are faithfully refreshed to preclude any stumbling blocks to a new generation of readers.

Man's Search for Himself - Rollo May

Signposts for living and personal fulfillment
Loneliness, boredom, emptiness: These are the complaints that Rollo May encountered over and over from his patients. In response, he probes the hidden layers of personality to reveal the core of man's integration - a basic and inborn sense of value. Man's Search for Himself is an illuminating view of our predicament in an age of overwhelming anxieties and gives guidance on how to choose, judge, and act during such times.

Jonathan Livingstone Seagull - Richard Bach

Jonathan Livingston Seagull, written by Richard Bach and illustrated by Russell Munson, is a fable in novella form about a seagull who is trying to learn about life and flight, and a homily about self-perfection. Jonathan Livingston Seagull is a simple story with a profound message. The message is that we can all be so much more than we believe, or are given to believe. That God - or fortune, if you wish - is on the side of the bold, the adventurous, and the free in spirit.
Bach wrote it as a series of short stories that were published in Flying magazine in the late 1960s. It was

first published in book form in 1970, and by the end of 1972 over a million copies were in print. Reader's Digest published a condensed version, and the book reached the top of the New York Times Best Seller list, where it remained for 37 weeks. In 1972 and 1973, the book topped the Publishers Weekly list of bestselling novels in the United States.

Build to Last - Jim Collins and Jerry I. Porras

"Built to Last: Successful Habits of Visionary Companies", is a book written by Jim Collins and Jerry I. Porras. It outlines the results of a six-year research project exploring what leads to enduringly great companies. The book is said to be "one of the most influential business books of our era".

The authors identified two primary objectives for the research published in the book: "to identify underlying characteristics are common to highly visionary companies" and "to effectively communicate findings so that they can influence management".

You are the Placebo - Dr. Joe Dispenza

Is it possible to heal by thought alone—without drugs or surgery? The truth is that it happens more often than you might expect. In "You Are the Placebo", Dr. Joe Dispenza shares numerous documented cases of those who reversed cancer, heart disease, depression, crippling arthritis, and even the tremors of Parkinson's disease by believing in a placebo. Similarly, Dr. Joe tells of how others have gotten sick and even died the victims of a hex or voodoo curse, or after being misdiagnosed with a fatal illness. Belief can be so strong that pharmaceutical companies use double- and triple-blind randomized studies to try to exclude the power of the mind over the body when evaluating new drugs.

Dr. Joe does more than simply explore the history and the physiology of the placebo effect. He asks the question: "Is it possible to teach the principles of the placebo, and without relying on any external substance, produce the same internal changes in a person's health and ultimately in his or her life?" Then he shares scientific evidence (including color brain scans) of amazing healings from his workshops, in which participants learn his model of personal transformation, based on practical applications of the so-called placebo effect. The book ends with a "how-to" meditation for changing beliefs and perceptions that hold us back— the first step in healing.

"You Are the Placebo", combines the latest research in neuroscience, biology, psychology, hypnosis, behavioral conditioning, and quantum physics to demystify the workings of the placebo effect and show how the seemingly impossible can become possible.

Breaking the habit of being yourself - Dr. Joe Dispenza

You are not doomed by your genes and hardwired to be a certain way for the rest of your life. New science is emerging that empowers all human beings to create the reality they choose. In Breaking the Habit of Being Yourself, renowned author, speaker, researcher, and chiropractor Dr. Joe Dispenza combines the fields of quantum physics, neuroscience, brain chemistry, biology, and genetics to show you what is truly possible.

Not only will you be given the necessary knowledge to change any aspect of yourself, but you will also be taught the step-by-step tools to apply what you learn to make measurable changes in any area of your life. Dr. Joe demystifies ancient understandings and bridges the gap between science and spirituality. Through his powerful workshops and lectures, thousands of people in 25 different countries have used these principles to change from the inside out. Once you break the habit of being yourself and truly change your mind, your life will never be the same!

The Secret - Rhonda Byrne

In 2006, a groundbreaking feature-length film revealed the great mystery of the universe, "The Secret" and, later that year, Rhonda Byrne followed with a book that became a worldwide bestseller.

"Fragments of a Great Secret" have been found in the oral traditions, in literature, in religions, and philosophies throughout the centuries. For the first time, all the pieces of "The Secret" come together in an incredible revelation that will be life-transforming for all who experience it.
In this book, you'll learn how to use The Secret in every aspect of your life, money, health, relationships, happiness, and in every interaction, you have in the world. You'll begin to understand the hidden, untapped power that's within you, and this revelation can bring joy to every aspect of your life.

"The Secret" contains wisdom from modern-day teachers, men and women who have used it to achieve health, wealth, and happiness. By applying the knowledge of The Secret, they bring to light compelling stories of eradicating disease, acquiring massive wealth, overcoming obstacles, and achieving what many would regard as impossible.

The Alchemist - Paulo Coelho
Paulo Coelho's enchanting novel has inspired a devoted following around the world. This story, dazzling in its powerful simplicity and soul-stirring wisdom, is about an

Andalusian shepherd boy named Santiago who travels from his homeland in Spain to the Egyptian desert in search of a treasure buried near the Pyramids. Along the way, he meets a Gypsy woman, a man who calls himself king, and an alchemist, all of whom point Santiago in the direction of his quest. No one knows what the treasure is, or if Santiago will be able to surmount the obstacles in his path. But what starts as a journey to find worldly goods turns into a discovery of the treasure found within. Lush, evocative, and deeply humane, the story of Santiago is an eternal testament to the transforming power of our dreams and the importance of listening to our hearts.

Awaken The Giant Within - Anthony Robbins

Wake up and take control of your life! From the bestselling author of "Inner Strength, "Unlimited Power", and "MONEY Master the Game", Anthony Robbins, the nation's leader in the science of peak performance, shows you his most effective strategies and techniques for mastering your emotions, your body, your relationships, your finances, and your life.
The acknowledged expert in the psychology of change, Anthony Robbins provides a step-by-step program teaching the fundamental lessons of self-mastery that will enable you to discover your true purpose, take control of your life and harness the forces that shape your destiny.

Screw It, Let's Do It: Lessons In Life - Richard Branson

"Throughout my life, I have achieved many remarkable things. In Screw It, Let's Do It, I will share with you my ideas and the secrets of my success, but not simply because I hope they'll help you achieve your individual goals.

Today we are increasingly aware of the effects of our actions on the environment, and I strongly believe that we each have a responsibility, as individuals and organisations, to not harm. I will draw on Gaia Capitalism to explain why we need to take stock of how we may be damaging the environment, and why it is up to big companies like Virgin to lead the way in a more holistic approach to business.

In "Screw It, Let's Do It", I'll be looking forwards to the future. A lot has changed since I founded Virgin in 1968, and I'll explain how I intend to take my business and my ideas to the next level and the new and exciting areas - such as launching Virgin Fuels - into which Virgin is currently moving.

But I have also brought together all the important lessons, good advice, and inspirational adages that have helped me along the road to success.

Ironically, I have never been one to do things by the book, but I have been inspired and influenced by many remarkable people. I hope that you too might find a little inspiration between these pages".

The Art of Happiness - Dalai Lama

Nearly every time you see him, he's laughing, or at least smiling. And he makes everyone else around him feel like smiling. He is the Dalai Lama, the spiritual and temporal leader of Tibet, a Nobel Prize winner, and an increasingly popular speaker and statesman. What's more, he'll tell you that happiness is the purpose of life, and that "the very motion of our life is towards happiness." How to get there has always been the question. He's tried to answer it before, but he's never had the help of a psychiatrist to get the message across in a context we can easily understand. Through conversations, stories, and meditations, the Dalai Lama shows us how to defeat day-to-day anxiety, insecurity, anger, and discouragement. Together with Dr. Cutler, he explores many facets of everyday life, including relationships, loss, and the pursuit of wealth, to illustrate how to ride through life's obstacles on a deep and abiding source of inner peace.

The science of getting rich - Wallace Wattles

As featured in the bestselling book, "The Secret", here is the landmark guide to wealth creation republished with the classic essay "How to Get What You Want." Wallace D. Wattles spent a lifetime considering the laws of success as he found them in the work of the world's great philosophers. He then turned his life effort into this simple, slender book – a volume that he vowed could replace libraries of philosophy, spirituality, and self-help to attain one definite goal: a life of prosperity. Wattles describes a definite science of wealth attraction, built on the foundation of one commanding idea: There is a thinking stuff from which all things are made. A thought, in this substance, produces the thing that is imaged by the thought." In his seventeen short, straight-to-the-point chapters, Wattles shows how to use this idea, how to overcome barriers to its application, and how to work with very direct methods that awaken it in your life. He further explains how creation and not competition is the hidden key to wealth attraction, and how your power to get rich uplifts everyone around you. "The Science of Getting Rich" concludes with Wattle's rare essay "How to Get Want You Want" – a brilliant refresher of his laws of wealth creation.

Falling Forward - John Maxwell
Failing Forward: Turning Mistakes into Stepping Stones for Success. These three lessons will help you to change your perspective. Even if a failure isn't your fault, take responsibility for your future success. The only way to

make failure useful is to learn from it. Focus on three things to make the most of the opportunities you get.

Unfu*k yourself - Gary John Bishop
Have you ever felt like a hamster on a wheel, furiously churning your way through life but somehow going nowhere? It seems like there's a barrage of information surrounding us in our everyday lives with the keys to this thing or that thing, be it wealth, success, happiness, or purpose. The truth is, most of it fails to capture what it truly takes to overcome our greatest barrier to a greater life…ourselves. What if everything you ever wanted is in you like a well of potential, waiting to be expressed? "Unfu*k Yourself" is the handbook for the resigned and defeated, a manifesto for real-life change and unleashing your greatness.

Life without limits - Nic Vujicic
"Life Without Limits" is an inspiring book by an extraordinary man. Born without arms or legs, Nick Vujicic overcame his disability to live not just independently but a rich, fulfilling life, becoming a model for anyone seeking true happiness. Now an internationally successful motivational speaker, his central message is that the most important goal for anyone is to find their life's purpose despite whatever difficulties or seemingly impossible odds stand in their way.

Nick tells the story of his physical disabilities and the emotional battle he endured trying to deal with them as a child, a teen, and a young adult. "For the longest, loneliest time, I wondered if there was anyone on earth like me and whether there was any purpose to my life other than pain and humiliation." He shares how his faith in God has been his central source of strength and explains that once he found his sense of purpose - inspiring others to make their lives and the world better -he found the confidence to build a rewarding and productive life without limits.

Nick offers practical advice for realising a life of fulfillment and happiness by building trust in others, developing supportive relationships, and gaining strength for the journey. He encourages the reader by showing how he learned to accept what he could not control and focus instead on what he could.

"I do believe my life has no limits! I want you to feel the same way about your life, no matter what your challenges may be. As we begin our journey together, please take a moment to think about any limitations you've placed on your life or that you've allowed others to place on it. Now think about what it would be like to be free of those limitations. What would your life be if anything were possible?"

The Royal Path of Life - Thomas Louis Haines, Levi W. Yaggy

The subject matter of this book, success and happiness, has been the consideration of every eminent pen, from the days of Solomon to the present. To say anything strictly new would be impossible; nor would be presumed that the authors' knowledge and experience would be as valuable as the maxims of the wise and sublime truths which have become a part of the standard literature. The best that anyone can expect to do is to recombine the experiences of the past, and compile such thoughts and extracts as have been chimed in with the testimony of earnest and aspiring minds and offer them in a novel and fascinating form.

The Four Agreements - Miguel Ruiz

In "The Four Agreements", Don Miguel Ruiz reveals the source of self-limiting beliefs that rob us of joy and create needless suffering. Based on ancient Toltec wisdom, the Four Agreements offer a powerful code of conduct that can rapidly transform our lives into a new experience of freedom, true happiness, and love. The Four Agreements are: Be Impeccable With Your Word, Don't Take Anything Personally, Don't Make Assumptions, Always Do Your Best.

Shoe Dog - Phil Knight

In this candid and riveting memoir, for the first time, Nike founder and CEO Phil Knight shares the inside story of the company's early days as an intrepid start-up and its evolution into one of the world's most iconic, game-changing, and profitable brands.

In 1962, fresh out of business school, Phil Knight borrowed $50 from his father and created a company with a simple mission: import high-quality, low-cost athletic shoes from Japan. Selling the shoes from the trunk of his lime-green Plymouth Valiant, Knight grossed $8,000 his first year. Today, Nike's annual sales top $30 billion. In an age of start-ups, Nike is the plus ultra of all start-ups, and the swoosh has become a revolutionary, globe-spanning icon, one of the most ubiquitous and recognizable symbols in the world today.

But Knight, the man behind the swoosh, has always remained a mystery. Now, for the first time, in a memoir that is candid, humble, gutsy and wry, he tells his story, beginning with his crossroads moment. At 24, after backpacking around the world, he decided to take the unconventional path, to start his own business—a business that would be dynamic, different.

Knight details the many risks and daunting setbacks that stood between him and his dream—along with his early triumphs. Above all, he recalls the formative relationships with his first partners and employees, a ragtag group of misfits and seekers who became a tight-knit band of brothers. Together, harnessing the transcendent power of a shared mission, and a deep belief in the spirit of sport, they built a brand that changed everything.

Man's Search for Meaning - Victor Frankl

Psychiatrist Viktor Frankl's memoir has riveted generations of readers with its descriptions of life in Nazi death camps and its lessons for spiritual survival. Based on his own experience and the stories of his patients, Frankl argues that we cannot avoid suffering but we can choose how to cope with it, find meaning in it, and move forward with renewed purpose.

At the heart of his theory, known as logotherapy, is a conviction that the primary human drive is not pleasure but the pursuit of what we find meaningful. "Man's Search for Meaning" has become one of the most influential books in America; it continues to inspire us all to find significance in the very act of living.

The Art of War - Sun Tzu

Twenty-five hundred years ago, Sun Tzu wrote this classic book of military strategy based on Chinese warfare and military thought. Since that time, all levels of the military have used the teaching of Sun Tzu on warfare. Civilization has adapted these teachings for use in politics, business and everyday life. The "Art of War" is a book that should be used to gain the advantage of opponents in the boardroom and battlefield alike.

Raise your vibrational frequency to what you want.
People blame their circumstances for their problems. Change that by working to get or create the circumstances you desire.
It doesn't matter what things are like, they can get better! That's what we want to put our focus on.

"The good you find in others is a reflection of the good that is yourself". Bob Proctor

I'm so happy and grateful now that I use life's challenges to learn, improve, better myself and grow stronger.

Everything happens when it's supposed to happen. Everything in this universe operates by law.

What you resist will persist. Because when you resist, you are directing negative energy towards what you are resisting, and when doing so, you make it harder for the problem to get resolved.

Pay attention to your body. When you are struggling with something, you are not letting things flow. You are blocking the flow of energy coming into you and out of you.

Resistance is created by our limiting beliefs or fears by our opinion of how something or someone should be. Learn to let go of the fears and limiting beliefs.
Trust.

Have faith that the universe is always working towards what's best for you.

We are not natural-born liars. Events in our lives make us scared and cowardly. Mostly it is our own bad decisions that make us lie or we lie on behalf of someone else. We lie to deceive, we lie to protect and we lie to hurt somebody.

Live your life in such a pure way so as not to land in a situation where you have to lie or twist the truth and do not associate with people who land you in situations where you have to lie for them. Never lie on behalf of somebody. It is not worth it and most probably they would not do the same for you.
Honesty is a universal value. We expect other human beings to be honest and we expect business people to offer honest service, yet we do not do the same.

To be honest, takes effort and integrity. You will always have to cover one lie with another unless you face up to and produce, the truth.

> "The only limits in our life are those we impose on ourselves". Bob Proctor

People can sense dishonesty in others. It is like you are what you eat. You cannot hide the fact if you overeat. What you have in your soul will manifest.

Greed is a huge contributing factor to lies. People backstab each other through lies to cheat each other out of deals. Lies are used as promises to deliver products or complete projects by a certain time to secure the deal and receive the money.

Always ensure that you are involved in transparent deals with honest people. Ensure that you know the background of the people you are dealing with.

You are better off with nothing rather than ending up losing your reputation, work, clients, friends, family and dignity.

What can other people do if you simply tell the truth?

Why do people, when they cheat, not have the guts to say, "I do not think I am comfortable with our relationship and do not want to hurt you".

You will surely hurt their feelings, but it will hurt them more to find out through lies and deception. You will lose the respect and trust of that person.

Be courageous and strong when you have to face uncomfortable situations and do not entertain the thought of telling a lie or twisting the truth. It is simply not worth it in the end.

People might not find out that you have lied, but it will fester in the foundation of your soul and manifest on your face.

Raise your energy by taking 15 minutes in the morning grooming yourself. Apply a bit of make-up or shave and dress in decent clothes, not just a tracksuit or something casual. Look successful and happy.

1. Set yourself a definite goal.
2. Stop running yourself down.
3. Stop thinking of all the reasons why you cannot be successful.
4. Trace your attitude to your childhood or where the idea of why you cannot be successful comes from.
5. Change the image you have of yourself by writing down what you want to be.
6. Act the part.

Have multiple money-earning ideas.

The only way to earn money is by providing a product or service people need and want. You can only earn money after you are successful. You have to work hard before you can earn money. The amount of money you have will be determined by the quality and quantity of the product or service you provide. Give the best and give more where you can.

> "It's a beautiful thing. You can take your pen and you can write something down and you know it's going to happen. You can predict what's going to happen in the future". Bob Proctor

I heard once that you should have multiple business ideas and try all of them or at least do your homework on each idea. If one idea fails then you have others. I also read that inventors write down at least ten ideas daily.

So, how do you know which business to start? How do you know if it will be right for you in the long run? My answer to this is for each idea, do the cash flow forecast. You must do this very realistically. Do not overestimate income but do a worst-case scenario. Get previous sales data. Do surveys. Go and observe the area in which you want to do business. Ensure that the products you want to sell will be regularly available. Ensure the service you want to offer is something that most people want and that you can do, come rain or sunshine.

> "I am not a product of my circumstances. I am a product of my decisions". Stephen Covey

There is no signal the universe will give you, meant just for you, as to when it is the right time to start a business or that it is the right business. Risk-takers do their homework and if there is a margin for success, they leap.
People see your success but they do not see the hard work, risk, late nights, struggles, failures, persistence, action, discipline, courage, doubts, changes, criticism, disappointments, adversity, rejection, and sacrifices that went into that success.

> "If you wait until you know how to do it, you'll never do it." Bob Proctor

Money is a reward received for services rendered. You can not make money, that is the task of The Mint. You earn money. The more services you render the more you're going to earn. Money is only an energy source. A great way to measure results is through money. You can count money to the cent. You cannot measure happiness or health. So what are your money results?

Why do you have what you have? Is it debt? Is it a lack of disposable income every month? Do you give your money, time and resources away to be in with the crowd or to be admired by hollow people, to your detriment?

A person does not earn only R100 000 a year because he wants to. He earns that because he does not know how to generate or earn R100 000 a month!

Expanding your awareness is simply putting a bigger idea in place of a smaller idea.

Save and Invest your money wisely.

Things we pay for, we value and things we get for free, well, we do not value. Everything in life which is worthwhile came as a standard issue in every human being. Our brain, our soul, our body amongst other great gifts were given to us at no cost. Not a cent. What do we do with these gifts? How do you apply these gifts? Think about it for a moment and make a mental list of the great or mindful things you have done with your gifts.

Any debt is a thief of joy and peace. It turns the most beautiful face to that of morbid sadness.

You can't love and be content whilst debt is watching you at your back door.

> "The only thing that separates a millionaire from you right now is a wealthy mindset, and the foundation of that mindset is belief." Bob Proctor

It is undeniable that food is expensive. Food can be bought on credit and people run up huge bills buying, ad-lib. The only man who sticks closer to you in adversity than a friend is a creditor.

In most cases debt is run up due to a need, but in other cases, it is run-up to "Keep up with the Joneses" - comparing yourself to your "neighbour" and trying to keep up your social acceptance through the accumulation of material goods. A new expensive car, on credit, will consume your money; money you could have invested to grow.

Just invest your money!

The golden rule is not to spend what you do not have.

Do not procrastinate.
Procrastination is the result of your goals not being linked to your higher values.

When you want something you will start and not quit.

If you have a set-back then you must go back, try and try again and get the T-shirt.

The people who made mistakes and learned from them, recovered, and made the paradigm shift successfully, are the ones you have to study and pay attention to.

> "I do not believe in going halfway in anything. You either go all the way or you don't do it". Bob Proctor

Discipline is the ability to give yourself a command and then follow it.
How difficult is it to command yourself? For me, it is the most difficult thing to do.

If you are disciplined, you can have anything you seriously want.

We have paradigms. A paradigm is a multitude of habits that are lodged in your subconscious mind. You must change the paradigm in the same way it was created - through the repetition of information. I have experienced that I have negative convictions about myself. So do others. We were told certain things about ourselves, by our parents, teachers, and friends. It stuck.

We see our parents drink and it becomes acceptable for us to drink. Nothing changes if we do not change and replace bad habits with good habits.

> "Commit to actively work toward your dream daily - make it a priority". Bob Proctor

Make an irrevocable commitment to discipline yourself. Start with de-cluttering your room, bathroom, kitchen, and other cluttered rooms. Donate all you do not want. This will also give you a sense of purpose and make you feel great. Dress neatly. Not just a tracksuit. Put make-up on and comb your hair in a new style. This will give you a sense of having control.

Give willingly and receive graciously.

The moment you have to think before you give, then it is not giving.

> "Be like a postage stamp, stick to it until you get there". Bob Proctor

You have to get to the point where you ignore all the reasons why you can't. Don't even spend five seconds thinking why you can't because you're giving negative energy to yourself. Only focus on how you can.
Your results are simply a reflection of your past thinking. There is no reason to be mad or upset if you are not satisfied with your current results. You've heard me say

this many times. My own life changed - that is, my external results changed - when my paradigms did.

Have emotional, physical, and financial boundaries.

Know what is happening around you. Be in control of what is happening within you.

When you do not set boundaries, everybody, except yourself, benefits. How strange is it when you start setting boundaries. People start marginalising you because they do not benefit anymore. They will get nasty and say "You have changed" or "You are the one being nasty".

Setting boundaries for yourself will feel strange in the beginning. You will start feeling isolated because the so-called friends will start to "disintegrate" and you will also be less popular, get fewer invites, and have fewer visits from friends.

Your boundaries are very important. When people walk all over you, you will start feeling inferior and not be able to say "no". You will not be able to prioritise and this will land you in all sorts of situations you do not want to be in.
You will end up spending money you did not need or want to, but the so-called 'friends' insisted on having

you with them, making you feel important and making you feel as though you belonged, as long as you paid for food and drinks.

You will end up wasting time that you could have used to advance yourself, your career, or your family - time you have spent going out with friends or having a party, ending up over-drinking and feeling miserable the next day. Not just because of the excessive alcohol but also feeling miserable to have allowed it.

There are personal boundaries too and these might be tougher to keep than you think. These are boundaries such as not over-eating, not over-drinking, not losing your temper, not smoking, not gossiping, not procrastinating or not indulging in illegal substances.

You need boundaries.

It will be very tough to face. Then, how do we keep these boundaries? Once you have crossed your boundary, hop back and understand what triggered you to cross it.

What was it that made you not care about that boundary? Write down what triggered you and add the date. Write how you felt and what the circumstances were before you crossed the boundary. Through this, you can analyse what happened, when you were "over" the indulgence, mood, or whatever it was.

Through this, you will realise that there is a grey area or a blurred area where you lose all your strength, willpower and determination. It is an area where you become blind or you blind yourself to the challenge you are facing and then you give in.

> "Your results are not according to your intellect or what you know on a conscious level, but they are according to your programming to your level of consciousness".
> Bob Proctor

Once you give in you cannot stop. If you have a big enough "reason" as to why you have set these boundaries, then you will snap out of this blind spot more quickly and you will have fewer lapses.

Ways to keep up your boundaries:

1. Feel how you felt when you crossed your boundary. Feel how disappointed you felt afterward. Do you want to feel like that again and again and again? Einstein's true words are relevant here: "Insanity is doing the same thing over and over and expecting different results."

2. When you experience your blind spot, think of your goal. Force yourself to think of it in that blind moment. Walk to a bathroom to get some privacy and look yourself in the mirror and remind yourself who and what

you really are. Tell yourself to be strong and that you can get through this and that you will get to the victory side.

3. If you know that you might be in a situation, put an elastic band around your wrist and snap it every time you feel weak or have an urge. You will tell yourself that you will not do this again. But then the friends call on you again for a good time and you have the fear of missing out (FOMO). Most of the time you will initiate the party, to have company, to feel popular and accepted.

The moment you start saying "no", you will see who your true friends are. They are the ones who will respect your choice, will also rather have a normal evening with you and respect you if you do not want to drink. The ones who do not respect your choice will call you a "pissy" or a "fader" and say that you are letting them down. These fake friends are the ones who will manipulate you emotionally, make you feel that you are not good enough. Try it and you will lose the "leeches". The true and respectful friends will stay.

At first, you will feel lonely and question whether you are doing the right thing. As you drink less, you will start feeling better emotionally and your bank balance will show that you are not spending your money on "empty" pleasure and "empty" friends. You will find a new lust for life. This will in turn make you set new goals for yourself.

After a while, when you start looking back, you will start noticing how blind you were to have allowed these leeches to suck up your energy, your money and your joy. You will realise that the joy you might have experienced during the "good" times you had was not real joy and you were only there to benefit them, while you were paying and giving whatever it was they wanted.

It is tough to set boundaries. It might take you some time, months, maybe even years, to realise that there are leeches in your life and that you have to stop them. Most people only realise it when they have lost everything and the leeches have disappeared because you do not have anything to offer anymore.

Then it is too late.

Get rid of the leeches now, protect your resources while you still have time. Set your boundaries by saying "no" to the parties, outings, or having them sitting at your bar, "drinking up" your time and money.

If you are at a point where you have lost everything, it is not too late to start over again, but with boundaries.

Take great care of yourself, your family, your time and your money. In the end, the parties are nice, but it is a deep dark well, which you are blindly falling into. Do not let the leeches take your livelihood away from you. Rather be alone for a while, build up a quality life and seek true and respectful friends.

Setting boundaries might be one of the most difficult emotional steps you will ever have to take, but it is the one thing that will save your life. Your boundaries will never fail you, but your friends will.

These days the biggest consumers of our time are WhatsApp, Facebook, Twitter, Instagram and e-mails.

We are distracted while we are busy with a task and we think nothing of it to just pick up our phone to attend to social media. If we don't, we will feel disconnected from the world or we will suffer from "FOMO"(Fear Of Missing Out).
If we have to write down the time we are spending on social media, then we will see how much time we have allowed being wasted— the time we could have spent with our children, spouses, or other family members.
If, for instance, you are busy with a task or studying, put your phone in another room or put it on flight mode. You will complete your task quickly and most likely deliver better quality work.

Spending time with people who drink and constantly gossip, steals the time you could have spent with family or devoted to a skills course, which would add value to your life.

Be mindful as to how you spend your time, on what and with whom. The more you spend your time on quality things the less important the rest becomes.

Acknowledge the mistakes you have made with your time and resources. Guard how you spend your time and with whom. Time is a commodity and runs out. Use it to benefit you. Think of how to use your time to improve your life. Think about it and write down your goals and the time it will take to reach them.

If you spend your time pleasing friends by spending your well-earned money on them, then you will end up sitting alone, without money.

Have a budget and use only the money you have budgeted for each expense and invest the rest in your old age and contingencies. The important thing is getting started right now! Whether you start with R50 a month or R100 a month or R500 per month, for every month you delay, you are losing thousands of rands on your old-age pension.

A little money invested consistently over a long period can yield a lot of money.

Let us look at what happens if you invest R100 every month for twenty years with a 7% return.

At the end of 20 years, you will have paid in R24 000, but you will have R52 093 in your account. What if, instead, you leave the money untouched for thirty years?

Still investing R100 per month, the investment pool will have grown to over R121 997.10. Not bad! We put aside R100 per month for 360 months, which would be R36000. But our R100 month investments earned almost R86 000, more than double the amount we put in!

How much would be there if the program runs for 40 years?

The investment pool is now up to R262 481.34. We put aside R100 per month for 480 months, which would be R48 000.

But our R100 a month investment earned almost R215 000! R262 500 invested at 7% would give an annual income of R18 375 per year without touching the investment pool. If you start at 20, at 60 you can have that income. Starting at 30 would allow withdrawal at 70. 40 would be at 80, etc. It is easy to see that the earlier the program is started, the earlier you can withdraw.

But a program at 50 will still get you there at 80, particularly if you double the money to R200. Just R200 a month, beginning at 50, will give you almost R244 000 at age 80 when you would need it.

Most of us know that schools teach us nothing about money. If this one idea would be repeated over and over again from primary school through to high school until it became part of the students' psyches, we would have a much better economy!

For example, a 19-year old (Investor A) opens a savings account with R2 000 at an average growth rate of 10% per year. After eight years this fellow makes no more contributions.

A second investor (Investor B) waits until age 26 (eight years later). He also makes a R2 000 contribution, but he continues to do so faithfully until age 65 and gets the same return.

Investor A ends up with more money than Investor B who contributed the entire time. Remember, Investor A only contributed R16 000, whereas Investor "B" contributed R80 000, almost five times more!

The compounding effect of the additional 8 years is phenomenal. It is never too early to start saving or investing. Good investors know that the earlier you start the more you end up with. Wealth creation is like climbing a mountain. It is much easier to start earlier and take a longer, but flatter, path than to wait till the last moment and try to sprint up the cliff face.

Use compounding to your advantage. Most people have heard of compounding, but do not understand the power of compounding. If they did, they would make entirely different financial decisions!

With compounding, money makes money, which in time makes even more money. Instead of withdrawing dividends or interest made by your investments, you add it back into your investment. You start earning interest on your interest. The good news is that the longer you give that process to grow, the faster it increases, which is why time and compounding work together to dramatically increase your wealth.

For example: if you had placed R10 000 into an account at a fixed interest rate of 8% per annum with the interest compounding every year, it would build up to R46 610 in 20 years. Let us imagine that you have a friend who also invested R10 000 on the same terms but with an interest rate of 16% per annum.
It would be logical to think that, at the end of the time, your friend would have twice what you have. After all, 16% is double 8%. It might be logical, but it would be incorrect. Your friend's R10 000 would have grown to

R194 607, while your investment would have only grown to R66 052. In this case, multiplying the rate by two, increased the return by more than four times. Is that not amazing?

This knowledge could be worth a lot of money.
Imagine that you and your friend both kept your money deposited for a further five years (so that the term became 25 years and not 20 years). Your investment would grow to

R68 484 and your friends' would have grown to R408 742.

During those extra five years, the dual effect of the period and the higher rate would have enabled your friend to grow his money six times larger than yours. The longer you stay invested, the more dramatic growth you see as a result of giving your investment and compounding, time to grow. As you can see, compounding works best the more time you give it. Build your wealth faster and start today. Some people never get to hear about the importance of time and rate on their investments. Yet this is the foundation of all wealth creation.

Understand how money works.
Most people have never studied finance or investing in school. To master anything, you have to understand it. Read. Study what successful people do.

Take classes or do a course. Master your relationship with money. Some of us spend for excitement, to show off, or to prove we can. Some of us are addicted to spending, and some of us are just careless about it. Whatever your relationship with money is, understand it, and develop a relationship of respect, appreciation and gratitude. Use your money, rather than allowing it to run your life. Understand and accept the cycles of money. The setbacks you may have today or next year will not keep you from financial freedom.

If you hold on to your goals and dreams, you will get there.

Most people fail to realise that, in life, it is not how much money you make, but rather how much money you keep. We have heard stories of lottery winners who became rich, suddenly, then poor again. They win millions and are soon back to where they started. If you want to become wealthy, you need to become financially literate. If you are going to build a house, the first thing you need to do is dig deep trenches and pour a strong foundation.

> "There is good in everything. The more you look for it, the more you're going to find". Bob Proctor

Begin to learn more about successful investing. Most of us spend or speculate. Both are roads to disaster! Learn to invest in things you understand. Learn to invest cautiously, wisely and regularly. The objective is not to "make a killing", but to get rich over time. Know and obey the distinction between gambling and putting your money to work for you. Learn to recognise true wealth.

Money itself will not make you financially free. That comes only as a result of a powerful state of mind, which tells us that we are worth far more than our money.

Your question for any plan should always be, "What if?".

That does not mean you are negative or scared. It shows that you are proactive. There are things in the environment that you cannot control. In 2020 we were hit by the Coronavirus and most people had not planned for the exhausting duration of the lockdown. Even for insignificant plans, you should have backup plans. For instance, if you go out at night with friends, and are dependent on their transport, have a friend or family on call to pick you up in case you miss your lift. Make sure your phone is fully charged when going out. Memorise important numbers in case your phone gets lost.

The wiser, older folk always believed in, "putting away money for a rainy day".

Remember, if you have a job at this stage: If you do not do more for what you are getting paid, you will never be paid for what you are doing. Money circulates through the economy from those who least value it, to those who value it the most. You have to value wealth building more than spending.

Having a contingency or savings account will take discipline to manage and is there to access only when it is truly needed. This account will give you the confidence to face any adversity. Be strong!

Everything which happened in your past happened for a reason to prepare you to do what you have to do.

All you want will come to you in its own way. Be patient, work hard, think and visualise. Act as if it is impossible to fail. Be sincere, have integrity, and treat others with dignity. Have your card in your pocket with your goal.

Do not fear, do not let petty things annoy you.

Ask, and it shall be given you; seek, and ye
shall find; knock, and it shall be opened unto you:
For every one that asketh receiveth; and he that seeketh
findeth, and to him that knocketh it shall be opened.
King James Version of the Bible Matthew 7: 7 - 8

Become the person you want to be. Never give up.

And finally - your daily checklist. Read this list every morning until this is part of your DNA.

- ✓ Get up early
- ✓ Be grateful for at least 10 things
- ✓ Think only of positive actions
- ✓ Think about what you are thinking about
- ✓ Study yourself and successful people
- ✓ Be kind
- ✓ Have integrity, even with the smallest of things
- ✓ Visualise how you want to be and look like and work daily towards it
- ✓ Focus on your realistic goals
- ✓ Be present - don't be in your head the whole time
- ✓ Have control over yourself and your circumstances
- ✓ Never let anyone make you feel unworthy
- ✓ Get out of your mind and on your feet
- ✓ You do not have to see the whole picture now but keep moving forward, one step at a time.
- ✓ Never give up

Some information I am sharing is copyrighted to the respective owners (original creators) and I don't claim any right or ownership to it. It is merely valuable information that I shared to the improvement of the reader. I have given credit to each source. Research to verify information has been done extensively. With great care, I have given credit to the authors, if I know who created the information. If I have shared anything that you own the copyright to, and want to get credit for it or have it removed from this book, please send an e-mail to lp@forbusiness.co.za.

Thank you.

everything **IS** somewhere

o https://www.luxurybonechina.com/what-is-fine-bone-china/
o https://www.garboglass.com/news/the-difference-between-crystal-glass-and-normal-glass-cup.html
o https://www.foodrepublic.com/2014/12/22/10-things-you-probably-didnt-know-about-potatoes/
o https://idahopotatomuseum.com/potato-facts/
o https://wikidiff.com/anger/temper
o http://uir.unisa.ac.za/bitstream/handle/10500/14146/disser tation_gcumisa_st.pdf;jsessionid=16233BB4B2BAFE0731A 956BC270DD11C?sequence=1
o 7 Hildagonda Duckitt, Hilda's where is it of recipes, p. 54. 8 Persoonlike inligting: me Edelgard Claassens, Waterkloofweg 241, Pretoria, 27 Januarie 1986. 9 Vgl. S.J.A. de Villiers, Kook en geniet, p. 237 (sponskluitjies). 10 Mary Kuttel, Hildagonda Duckitt's book of recipes, p. 21; S. van H. Tulleken, Die praktiese kookboek vir Suid-Afika, p. 284. 11 Hildagonda Duckitt, Hilda's where is it of recipes, p. 55. 12 Henriëtte Davidis, Keukenboek, p. 121. Sy noem doekpoeding Jan-in -die-sak, ketel- of trommelkoek. 13 S. Niemandt, Tydskrif vir volkskunde en volkstaal, September 1984, 40/3, p. 51.
o https://www.mind.org.uk/information-support/tips-for-everyday-living/loneliness/about-loneliness/
o https://www.uky.edu/~eushe2/Pajares/OnFailingG.html#: ~:text=Thomas%20Edison's%20teachers%20said%20he, at%20inventing%20the%20light%20bulb.
o https://www.kitchenproject.com/history/PuffPastry.htm#: ~:text=Puff%20Pastry%20was%20invented%20in,of%20 water%2C%20flour%20and%20butter.

www.ingramcontent.com/pod-product-compliance
Lightning Source LLC
Chambersburg PA
CBHW051432090426
42737CB00014B/2930